A Monk, a Pilgrim, and the Purpose of Life

BROTHER JOHN

AUGUST TURAK

with paintings at Mepkin Abbey by

GLENN HARRINGTON

CP

Brother John

© 2018 by August Turak

Published by Clovercroft Publishing, Franklin, Tennessee

Paintings and Book Design by Glenn Harrington

Paintings © 2018 by Glenn Harrington

Edited by Lee Titus Elliott

Printed in Korea

ISBN   978-1-945507-94-6

Clovercroft|Publishing

Dedications

For Brother John and all my brothers of Mepkin Abbey

A. T.

For Mepkin Abbey, a profoundly beautiful place to be still and experience the magnificent handiwork of God.

G. H.

Preface

I will never forget the day that he came striding into my gothic office in the Duke University Chapel.

That day I encountered one of God's most curious, surprising, and challenging creations—Augie Turak. Intense yet warm, disarmingly direct but unthreatening, both reflective and passionate. I've met many people over the years; very few are as unforgettable.

In a few minutes, I heard how Augie, while earning a college degree, had recklessly read himself into the wisdom of Plato, Aristotle, Aquinas, Pascal, St. John of the Cross, Huang Po, and anybody else who might help him get to the bottom of life's meaning and purpose. Later, even as a businessman and successful entrepreneur, Augie had never abandoned his quest for Plato's life worth living. Now he told me he felt called to pass on what he had learned to college students so they wouldn't "get college but miss wisdom."

Soon, Augie organized the Self Knowledge Symposium (SKS) to help students "learn how to live a life of meaning and purpose." From North Carolina State University, to Duke University, to the University of North Carolina at Chapel Hill, the SKS student groups spread like wildfire. One of the most memorable teaching experiences of my life was spending an evening with Augie's SKS students at the University of North Carolina. My speaking invitation read: "Share what you have learned about life and God." A few months later, three hundred students listened attentively, and then eagerly bombarded me with questions for the next three hours. At eleven o'clock I finally pled, "I've got to go home. I'm too old for this much intellectual intensity!"

The SKS student groups were the organizational embodiment of Augie's character: Socrates on steroids.

Now we will meet Brother John: the Trappist monk who spiritually takes Augie by the hand during the most difficult time of his life; the friend and teacher who leads him on the journey to God and self that he could never have made on his own. It is Brother John who finally reveals the secret to the meaningful life that Augie had been searching for all his life.

Augie loves to be born again, and then again, in his constant quest for fresh, life-changing truth. He was therefore a perfect student for the best of teachers. Now in the same spirit that sent him to my office over twenty years ago, Augie feels called to share this wisdom with you. From Brother John, Augie learned: "We must commit to facing our doubts, limitations, and self-contradictions head-on while holding on to this voice of eternity." In the eternal silence of Mepkin Abby, Augie heard the still, small voice that leads us all toward eternal truth. I believe that God was in it.

Kathleen Norris, in her memoir, *The Cloister Walk*, gave us one of the most appreciative and informative looks at the special gifts of monastic life. Now, with *Brother John*, August Turak does the same.

This is a beautiful book beautifully illustrated by Glenn Harrington about a restless, ever-seeking mind under the influence of a beautiful man of God. Augie was dramatically changed by his encounter with Brother John, I'm sure that you will be, too.

—Will Willimon

Dr. Willimon, the former Dean of the Duke University Chapel, is a theologian and bishop in the United Methodist Church. He is currently Professor of the Practice of Christian Ministry at Duke Divinity School.

Introduction

In 2004, a former student urged me to enter the John Templeton Foundation "Power of Purpose"

Essay Contest. Answering the question, "What is the Purpose of Life?" in 3,500 words or less was

daunting enough, but I quickly discovered that I was also a novice writer going up against thousands

of professionals and previously published material. And just to keep it interesting, by the time I heard

about the year-long contest, the deadline was a mere ten days away.

I wasted several days writing furiously and getting nowhere. Then another former student came to

my rescue: "Why don't you just write up that story about Brother John and his magical umbrella

that you love telling so much?" One week later, and only hours before the deadline, I hit "send" and

submitted my essay. I was proud of *Brother John*. While I was quite certain I would not win the contest,

I felt I had, almost accidentally, finally said something important about Brother John. Something that

I had wanted to say for a very long time. Then, I forgot all about it.

Eight months later, I answered the phone, only to discover that I was on a conference call with five

or six people from the Templeton Foundation. They seemed to be trying to tell me—all at once, as

I recall—that *Brother John* had won the $100,000 grand prize! Initially, I suspected that friends were

playing a practical joke, but as the call devolved into a seemingly endless loop of me screaming "No!"

as they shouted "Yes!" I was finally convinced that *Brother John* had won.

A few weeks later, the award ceremony was held at New York City's fabled Four Seasons Restaurant. The keynote speech (as well as my $100,000 check!) was delivered by one of the contest's judges: Rick Warren, the best-selling author of *The Purpose Driven Life*. The wonderful people from the Templeton Foundation offered to fly Brother John to New York for the ceremony, and Father Francis, Mepkin Abbey's abbot, in a highly unusual dispensation, graciously allowed him to attend. Brother John's gentle demeanor and Irish sense of humor promptly stole the show. But perhaps best of all, my father, whose health was already rapidly failing, was able to attend, as well.

The Templeton Prize dramatically changed my life. *Brother John* was published in two anthologies, *The Best Christian Writing* and *The Best Catholic Writing*, and this, in turn, launched me on a second career. I became a leadership contributor for Forbes.com, an on-air radio contributor for the BBC, and Columbia Business School published my book, *Business Secrets of the Trappist Monks*. But the common fourteen-year-old thread that runs through all this subsequent work is the spirit of *service and selflessness*: a monastic thread that leads right back to a spool called *Brother John*.

But, despite my intense gratitude, over the years, *Brother John* gradually became a Zen koan for me: a frustrating stone in my shoe that led directly to this book. Let me explain.

Brother John was written in 2004, and it is increasingly hard to find, yet I still receive a small, but steady, stream of correspondence from people who have stumbled upon the essay. Almost without exception, they write about how *Brother John* helped them through the death of a child, an episode of severe depression, or a particularly painful divorce.

Being periodically reminded of the healing power of *Brother John* has been a double-edged blessing. I am, of course, profoundly moved and humbled by these letters. They always take me back to 1996: the year when the events you are about to read about actually took place. It was not an innocent religious "retreat" that initially sent me to Mepkin Abbey and Brother John. A freakish sky-diving accident had triggered a personal crisis, or "Dark Night of the Soul." I arrived at Mepkin Abbey hip deep in a desperate battle against depression, panic, and incipient despair. As a result, it has been especially gratifying to discover that my essay seems to convey a bit of that same healing power that I received from Brother John and the monks of Mepkin: a healing power that saved my life.

Yet there is also a downside to this blessing. Why? Because these letters always left me wondering how much more good *Brother John* could accomplish if it were more widely available. I seemed to be the proud owner of a marvelous candle snugly nestled under the proverbial bushel basket.

All this came to a head when a business executive drove 400 miles to thank me for writing *Brother John*. For several years, I had been toying with the idea of turning *Brother John* into an illustrated book. A busy executive willing to drive 400 miles proved decisive: something bigger than me was insisting that I act on my idea. Through grace or luck, I was able to find an amazing artist, collaborator, and friend in Glenn Harrington.

Glenn is an award-winning artist who has done illustrations and cover art for all the major publishers. He was also commissioned to paint many of the portraits that now grace the World Golf Hall of Fame. Glenn took immediately to the essay and to the project. On his own initiative, he travelled to Mepkin Abbey to meet Brother John and to immerse himself in the Trappist way of life. Glenn is a deeply religious man, and I believe that his art not only captures the spirit of *Brother John* but also conveys the serenity and mystical power that make Mepkin Abbey a spiritual nexus, a place where heaven and earth meet.

At the awards ceremony in New York City, I was asked what I intended to do with the $100,000 grand prize. I replied that I intended to give it to charity. After donating to Mepkin Abbey and several other favorite charities, I used the remainder to fund and form the Self Knowledge Symposium Foundation (SKSF).

The SKSF is a not-for-profit corporation we created. Our mission is to bring Brother John's transformative message of meaning and purpose to a Western culture increasingly bereft of meaning and purpose.

Over the intervening years, I continue to fund the SKSF, and any remuneration I receive from my writing, speaking engagements, consulting, or personal coaching, is donated back to the SKSF to underwrite our ongoing efforts. This book is our latest effort to make a difference, and the rights to my essay, and therefore to this book, have been transferred to the SKSF. All royalties will be reinvested into future efforts like this one. At the most critical moment of my life, Brother John offered to share his umbrella with me. My life is now dedicated to sharing, to the best of my ability, his magical umbrella with you and all my fellow men.

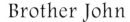

Brother John

In any case, I feel I can personally guarantee
that St. Thomas Aquinas loved God,
because for the life of me I cannot help loving St. Thomas.

- Flannery O'Connor

Uncertainty as to life's purpose is much in vogue today. So, too, are the relativistic notions that would consign life's purpose to a matter of taste. The agony of life is uncertainty, and the rationalization is that uncertainty is certain. However, the plain truth is that, for all our anguish, we treasure uncertainty. Doubt forestalls action. The problem with life's purpose is that we know damn well what it is but are unwilling to face the changes in our lives that a commitment to self-transcendence, to being the best human being we could possibly be, would entail. It wearies us just thinking about it. So we rationalize that it's all "relative," or that we're already doing enough and don't have time. Worst of all, we rationalize that those who do accept the challenges inherent in self-transcendence are uniquely gifted and specially graced.

It was eight in the evening on Christmas Eve, and I was waiting for Mass to begin. This was my second Christmas retreat at Mepkin Abbey monastery and my second Christmas Eve Mass. Mepkin Abbey sits on 3,132 acres, shaded by towering mossy oaks running along the Cooper River, just outside Charleston, South Carolina. Once the estate of Henry and Clare Boothe Luce, it is now a sanctuary for thirty or so Trappist monks living a life of contemplative prayer according to the arduous Rule of St. Benedict.

Already eighteen days into my retreat, I was finally getting used to getting up at three in the morning for the monastic service of Vigils. However, I also knew that, by the time this special evening Mass ended at 10:30, it would be well after our usual bedtime of eight o'clock. The church was hushed and dark, and two brothers began lighting the notched candles lining the walls, as Gregorian chant, sung by the hidden choir, wafted in from the chapel. This chapel, a favorite meditation spot for the monks, sits just off the main sanctuary.

The magic of these pre-Mass rituals quickly had me feeling like I was floating just above my seat. Soon I was drifting back to my first service ever at Mepkin, when Brother Robert, catching me completely off guard, urgently whispered from his adjacent stall, "The chapel is open all night!"

This man, a chapel denizen who sleeps barely three hours a night, was apparently so convinced that this was the answer to my most fervent prayer that all I could do was nod knowingly, as if to say, "Thank God!"

The sound of the rain pelting down on the copper roof of the church on this cold December evening drew me from my reveries, and I noticed, with the trace of a smile, that I was nervous. I had calmly lectured to large audiences many times, yet I was, as usual, worried that I would somehow screw up the reading that Brother Stan had assigned me for Mass. But reading at Mepkin, especially at Christmas, is such an honor.

I felt that my reading came off very well. Returning to my seat, I guess I was still excited, because, heedless of the breach of etiquette that speaking at Mass implied, I leaned over and asked Brother Boniface for his opinion. Brother Boniface is Mepkin's ninety-one-year-old statesman, barber, baker, and stand-up comic. He manages these responsibilities despite a painful arthritis of the spine that has left him doubled over and reduced his walk to an inching shuffle. Swiveling his head on his short, bent body in order to make eye contact, Boniface lightly touched my arm with his gnarled fingers and gently whispered through his German accent, "You could've been a little slower—and a little louder."

After Mass, I noticed that the rain had stopped. I headed
for the little Christmas party for monks and guests in the
dining hall, or refectory. Mepkin is a Trappist, or Cistercian,
monastery, and its official name, "The Order of the Cistercians
of the Strict Observance (OCSO)," is taken seriously. Casual
talking is actively discouraged, and even the vegetarian meals
are eaten in strict silence. Parties are decidedly rare—and not
to be missed.

The party was a fine affair, consisting of light conversation,
mutual Christmas wishes, and various Boniface-baked cookies
and cakes, along with apple cider. Mostly I just basked in the
glow of congeniality that I had come to associate so well with
Mepkin.

I didn't stay long. It was almost midnight, and, after a long day
of eight church services, packing eggs, mopping floors, feeding
logs into the wood-burning furnace, and helping Father
Guerric put up Christmas trees, I was asleep on my feet.

I said my good-byes and headed for my room several hundred yards away. Halfway to the refectory door, I heard the resurgent rain banging on the roof, reminding me that I had forgotten to bring an umbrella. Opening the door, I was cursing and resigning myself to a miserable hike and a wet monastic guest habit for morning services, when something startled me and left me squinting into the night. As my eyes adjusted, I made out a dim figure standing under an umbrella, outlined by the rain and glowing in the light from the still-open door. It was Brother John in a thin monastic habit, his slouched sixty-year-old body ignoring the cold.

"Brother John! What are you doing?"

"I'm here to walk the people who forgot their umbrellas back to their rooms," he replied softly.

Flicking on his flashlight, we wordlessly started off, sharing that single umbrella. For my part, I was so stunned by this timely offer that I couldn't speak. For in a monastery whose Cistercian motto is "prayer and work" and where there are no slackers, no one works harder than Brother John. He rises before three in the morning to make sure coffee is there for everyone, and is still working after most of his brethren have retired.

Brother John is also what might be termed Mepkin's foreman. After morning Mass, the monks without regular positions line up in a room off the church for work assignments, and, with several thousand acres full of buildings, machinery, and a farm with 40,000 chickens, there is plenty to do. (As a daily fixture at the grading house, packing and stacking eggs thirty dozen to a box, I could easily skip this ritual. I never do. Perhaps it is the way Brother John lights up when I reach the front of the line, touches me ever so lightly on the shoulder, and whispers "grading house" that brings me back every morning. Perhaps it is the humility I feel when he thanks me, as if I were doing him a personal favor.) Yet Brother John keeps it all in his head. Replacing every lightbulb that flickers out somewhere is his responsibility. He supervises when possible and delegates where he can, but as he is always shorthanded, he is constantly jumping in himself at some critical spot. Throughout the monastery, the phones ring incessantly, with someone on the line asking, "Is John there?" or, "Have you seen John?" And through it all, his Irish good humor and gentleness never fades or even frays.

Now, after just such a day, four hours after his usual bedtime, and forty years into his monastic hitch, here was Brother John eschewing Boniface's baking, a glass of cider, and a Christmas break in order to walk me back to my room under a shared umbrella.

When we reached the church, I reassured him several times that I could cut through to my room on the other side, before he relented. But as I opened the door of the church, something made me turn, and I continued to watch his flashlight as he hurried back for another pilgrim until its glow faded into the night. When I reached my room, I guess I wasn't as sleepy as I thought. I sat on the edge of my bed in the dark for what I can say, with some conviction, was a very long time.

Over the next week, I went about my daily routine at Mepkin as usual, but inside I was deeply troubled. I was obsessed with Brother John. On one hand, he represented everything I had ever longed for, and, on the other, all that I had ever feared. I'd read Christian mystics say that God is both terrible and fascinating, and, for me, Brother John had become both.

Of course, my obsession had nothing to do with the fact that he was a monk and I was not. On the contrary, Brother John was fascinating precisely because I intuited that to live as he did, to have his quiet peace and effortless love, had nothing to do with being a monk and was available to us all.

But Brother John was also terrible because he was a living, breathing witness to my own inadequacies. Like Alkibiades in Plato's *Symposium*, speaking of the effect Socrates had on him, I had only to picture Brother John under his umbrella to feel as if "life is not worth living the way I live it." I was terrified that if I ever did decide to follow the example of Brother John, I would either fail completely or, at best, be faced with a life of unremitting effort without Brother John's obvious compensations. I imagined dedicating my life to others, to self-transcendence, without ever finding that inner spark of eternity that so obviously made Brother John's life the easiest and most natural life I had ever known. Perhaps his peace and effortless love were not available to all, but only to some. Perhaps I just didn't have what it takes.

Finally, I asked Father Christian if he could spare a few minutes. Father Christian is Mepkin's feisty, eighty-eight-year-old former abbot, and my irreplaceable spiritual director. Slight and lean, his head is shaven, and he wears a bushy, chest-length beard, which he never cuts. When I commented that his beard didn't seem to be getting any longer, he regretfully said that his beard had stopped growing and added, "While, in the popular mind, the final length of my beard depends on my longevity, in actuality, it depends on my genetics." Fluent in French and Latin and passable in Greek, he acquired PhDs in Philosophy, Theology, and Canon Law as a Franciscan before entering Mepkin. His learning, his direct yet gentle manner, and his obvious personal spirituality make him an exceptional spiritual director. And while he grouses once in a while about the bottomless demand for his direction, I've never known him to turn anyone away.

I told Father Christian of my experience with Brother John, and I told him that it had left me in an unsettled state. I wanted to elaborate, but he interrupted me. "So you noticed, did you? Amazing how many people take something like that for granted in life. John's a saint, you know."

Then, seeming to ignore my predicament, he launched into a story about a Presbyterian minister having a crisis of faith and leaving the ministry. The man was a friend of his, and Father Christian took his crisis so seriously that he actually left the monastery and traveled to his house in order to do what he could. The two men spent countless hours in fruitless theological debate. Finally dropping his voice, Father Christian looked the man steadily in the face and said, "Bob, is everything in your life all right?" The minister said everything was fine. But the minister's wife called Father Christian a few days later. She had overheard his question and her husband's answer, and she told Father Christian that the minister was having an affair and was leaving her, as well as his ministry.

Father Christian fairly spat with disgust and said, "I was wasting my time. Bob's problem was that he couldn't take the contradiction between his preaching and his living. So God gets the boot. Remember this: all philosophical problems are at heart moral problems. It all comes down to how you intend to live your life."

We sat silently for a few minutes, while Father Christian cooled off. Maybe he finally took pity on the guy, or maybe it was something he saw in my face, but when he spoke, the anger in his clear, blue eyes had been replaced by a gentle compassion. "You know, you can call it original sin; you can call it any darn thing you want to, for that matter, but, deep down inside, every one of us knows something's twisted. Acknowledging that fact, refusing to run away from it, and deciding to deal with it is the beginning of the only authentic life there is. All evil begins with a lie. The biggest evil comes from the biggest lies, and the biggest lies are the ones we tell ourselves. And we lie to ourselves because we're afraid to take ourselves on."

Getting up from his chair, he went to a file cabinet in the corner of his office and took out a folded piece of paper. Turning, he handed it to me and said, "I know how you feel. You're wondering if you have what it takes. Well, God and you both have some work to do, but I'll say this for you: you're doing your best to look things square in the face."

As he walked out the door, I opened the paper he had given me. There, neatly typed by his ancient manual typewriter on plain white paper, was my name in all caps, followed by these words from Pascal:

> You would not seek Me if you had not already found Me,
>
> and you would not have found Me if I had not first found you.

On close inspection, so much of our indecisiveness concerning life's purpose is little more than a variation on the minister's so-called theological doubts. Ultimately, it is fear that holds us back, and we avoid this fear through rationalization. We are afraid that if we ever did commit to emulating the Brother Johns of the world, we would merely end up like the Presbyterian minister: pulled apart between the poles of how we *are* living and how we *ought* to live and unable to look away. We are afraid that if we ever did venture out, we would find ourselves with the worst of both worlds. On one hand, we would learn too much about life to return to our comfortable illusions, and, on the other, we would learn too much about ourselves to hope for success.

However, in our fear, we forget the miraculous.

This fear of the change we need to make in our lives reminds me of an old friend who, though in his thirties and married for some time, was constantly fighting with his wife over her desire to have a baby. Every time he thought of changing into a father, the walls closed in. Fatherhood, he thought, was nothing more than dirty diapers, stacks of bills, sleepless nights, and doting in-laws in every spare bed and couch. Fatherhood meant an end to spontaneous weekends and evenings with the guys. It also meant trading in his sports car for a minivan and a bigger life insurance policy. It was all so overwhelming.

Then one day he gave in. He set his jaw and made the decision to transform himself from a man into a father. He took the chance that he would find himself with all the responsibility of fatherhood and with none of its compensations. Then, on another day, his wife handed him his newborn boy.

.

Unexpectedly, an inner alchemy began, and something came over him from a direction he didn't know existed. He melted, and, magically, the baby gave birth to a father. He was so full of love for this child that he didn't know what to do with himself. While he once feared losing sleep, he began checking his baby so often that the baby lost sleep. He found himself full of boundless gratitude for his rebirth, regret for the fool he had been, and compassion for single friends who simply couldn't understand. He called it a miracle.

Similarly, we must take a chance and act on faith. We must give in, make the commitment, and be willing to pay the price. We must commit to becoming one with that passive spark of divinity longing for actuality that Thornton Wilder in *Our Town* describes so well:

> *Now there are some things we all know but we don't take'm out and look at'm very often. We all know that something is eternal . . . everybody knows in their bones that something is eternal and that something has to do with human beings. All the greatest people ever lived have been telling us that for five thousand years and yet you'd be surprised how people are always losing hold of it. There's something way down deep that's eternal about every human being.*

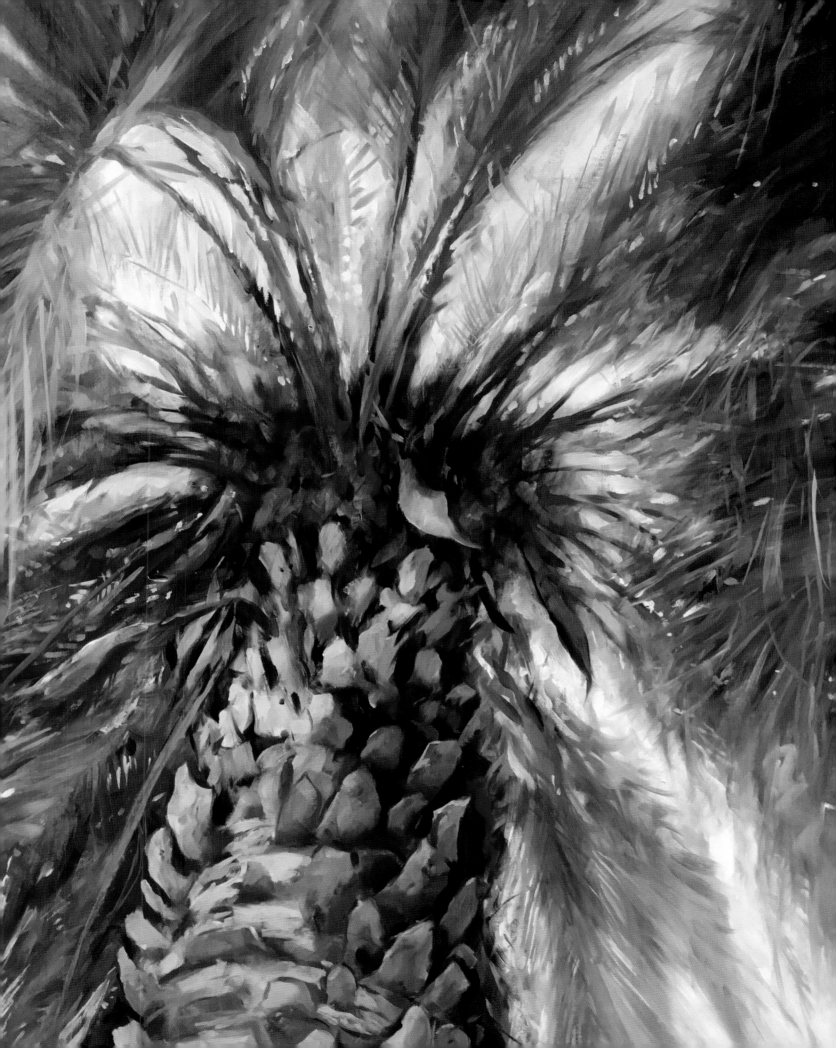

We must commit to facing our doubts, limitations, and self-contradictions head-on, while holding onto this voice of eternity. This eternal voice is urging us to take a chance on an unknown outcome in much the same way that nature's voice urged my friend to take a chance on a new life. And we must fight distraction, futility, rationalization, and fatigue at every step.

From this side of the chasm, we may react with dismay at all the work involved in never again "losing hold of it." From this side, it may be hard to imagine that, just as changing a diaper can be magically transformed from drudgery to an effortless privilege, so can standing outside in the rain for others. But, to experience the magic of this transformation, we must put aside these doubts. We must resolve to act decisively, while trusting in the aid of something we don't understand and can never predict. We must open ourselves up to the miraculous, to grace.

Working toward this miraculous transformation, rebirth, or inner alchemy is the true purpose of life. This transformation is what the West calls "conversion" and the East "enlightenment," and is the fruit of our commitment to the authentically purposeful life that Father Christian described so well. It is this transformation that turns work into effortless privilege, makes the unnatural values of Brother John second nature, and proves that the answer to the monks' last prayer each night at Compline for a "restful night and a peaceful death" is eternally ours. And when we're ready, Brother John will be waiting for us, eager to share this miraculous umbrella. Like him, we will be utterly grateful for who we have become, remorseful for who we were, and compassionate towards those who do not understand.

I am not a monk, but I spend enough time at Mepkin Abbey that Father Feliciano introduced me to a visitor recently and followed his introduction with, "He's always here." I am often asked why I go. I go because Brother John loves God so much he doesn't know what to do with himself. He doesn't know what to do with himself, so he stands outside on a cold Christmas night with an umbrella, waiting. Waiting to offer us some protection and human comfort on our long journey home.

JOURNAL

JOURNAL

JOURNAL

JOURNAL

Glenn Harrington's *original oils from*

BROTHER JOHN

All original oil paintings are painted on linen and framed in a custom carved Madary frame.

"Brother John"
Cover
26"x 30"

$ 12,000

"Spanish Moss"
Front Endpaper
12'x 18"

$ 6,500

"Mepkin at Night"
Title Page back endpaper

16"x 20"

SOLD

"Chapel"
Preface page 4

10"x 8"

$3,750

"Monks in Chapel"
page 13
24"x 20"

$ 11,000

"Candle Lighting"
pages 14-15
12"x 24"

$6,900

"August Reading"
page 16
17"x 20"

$7,500

"Christmas Party"
page 18
20'x 24"

$10,500

"August and John"
page 21
18"x 21"

$8,500

"John in Chapel"
page 22
24"x 20"

$10,500

To purchase original artwork from **Brother John,** please contact Melissa Hawks at:

Melissa@AugustTurak.com

252-204-1725

The Self Knowledge Symposium

All paintings are custom framed oil on linen originals and signed by Glenn Harrington

"Chapel Candle"

page 24
10"x 12"

$3,750

"Monk in Chapel"

page 27
16"x 18"

$6,500

"Cooper River"

pages 28-29
12"x18"

$6,900

"Hooded Monk"

page 31
16"x 20"

$7,500

"John in Garden"

page 32
16"x20"

$7,500

"Magnolia"

page 34
8"x10"

$3,750

"Mepkin Palm"

page 37
18"x24"

$9,800

"Mepkin Garden"

pages 38-39
"18"x24"

$9,800

"John and Cedar"

page 40
18"x24"

$8,500

"Mepkin Live Oak"

page 42
12"x24"

$6,900

"Mepkin Chapel Candle"

page 44
16"x 20"

$7,500

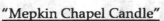

"Mepkin Monk"

dust Jacket
13"x 18"

$6,900